12/00 B+T 22.95

W9-BYZ-254

The Mildenhall Treasure

THIS IS A BORZOI BOOK PUBLISHED BY ALFRED A. KNOPF, A DIVISION OF RANDOM HOUSE, INC.

Text copyright © 1977 by Felicity Dahl and the other executors of the Estate of Roald Dahl
Illustrations copyright © 1999 by Ralph Steadman

All rights reserved under International and Pan-American Copyright
Conventions. Published in the United States by
Alfred A. Knopf, a division of Random House, Inc., New York,
and simultaneously in Canada by Random House of Canada Limited, Toronto.

Distributed by Random House, Inc., New York. Originally published
in different form in the United States in the collection
The Wonderful Story of Henry Sugar and Six More
by Alfred A. Knopf, a division of Random House, Inc., in 1977.

This edition originally published in 1999 in Great Britain by
Jonathan Cape Ltd., a division of Random House UK.
KNOPF, BORZOI BOOKS, and the colophon are registered trademarks of Random House, Inc.

www.randomhouse.com/kids

Library of Congress Cataloging-in-Publication Data
Dahl, Roald.
The Mildenhall treasure / Roald Dahl ; illustrated by Ralph Steadman.
p. cm.
SUMMARY: Describes how a British plowman unearthed a collection of Roman
silver in the 1940s and the events that followed this tremendous discovery.
ISBN 0-375-81035-8
1. Mildenhall (Suffolk, England)—Antiquities, Roman—Juvenile literature.
2. Silverware—England—Mildenhall (Suffolk)—Juvenile literature.
3. Romans—England—Mildenhall (Suffolk)—Juvenile literature.
[1. Mildenhall (Suffolk, England)—Antiquities, Roman.
2. Buried treasure.] I. Steadman, Ralph, ill. II. Title.
DA147.M64 D35 2000
936.2´643—dc21 00-024683

First Borzoi Books edition: September 2000

Printed in Singapore
10 9 8 7 6 5 4 3 2 1

NORTHBOROUGH FREE LIBRARY
NORTHBOROUGH, MA 01532-1997

ROALD DAHL
The Mildenhall Treasure

Pictures by

Ralph STEADman

Mildenhall market & Mr Butcher goes home after unearthing the biggest finds of Roman Gold in English History.

ALFRED A. KNOPF ❧ NEW YORK

W.J. Ford's engineering works, *c.* 1906. Left to right: -?-, Ted Ford, Cornelius Brown, Clark Brown, Sydney Ford, George Butcher, Noakes Ford and William Ford whose children are at the front. The Burrell Boydell engine of about 1857 is in for repair. The famous Mildenhall Treasure, a hoard of Roman silver now in the British Museum, was

A Note About This Story

IN 1946, more than thirty years ago, I was still unmarried and living with my mother. I was making a fair income by writing two short stories a year. Each of them took four months to complete, and fortunately there were people both at home and abroad who were willing to buy them.

One morning in April of that year, I read in the newspaper about a remarkable find of Roman silver. It had been discovered four years before by a plowman near Mildenhall, in the county of Suffolk, but the discovery had for some reason been kept secret until then. The newspaper article said it was the greatest treasure ever found in the British Isles, and it had now been acquired by the British Museum. The name of the plowman was given as Gordon Butcher.

True stories about the finding of really big treasure send shivers of electricity all the way down my legs to the soles of my feet. The moment I read that story, I leaped up from my chair without finishing my breakfast and shouted good-bye to my mother and rushed out to my car. The car was a nine-year-old Wolseley, and I called it "The Hard Black Slinker." It went well but not very fast.

Mildenhall was about a hundred and twenty miles from my home, a tricky cross-country trip along small twisty roads and country lanes. I got there at lunchtime, and by asking at the local police station, I found the small house where Gordon Butcher lived with his family. He was at home having his lunch when I knocked on his door.

I asked him if he would mind talking to me about how he found the treasure.

"No, thank you," he said. "I've had enough of reporters. I don't want to see another reporter for the rest of my life."

"I'm not a reporter," I told him. "I'm a short-story writer and I sell my work to magazines. They pay good money." I went on to say that if he would tell me exactly how he found the treasure, then I would write a truthful story about it. And if I was lucky enough to sell it, I would split the money equally with him.

In the end, he agreed to talk to me. We sat for several hours in his little kitchen, and he told me an enthralling story. When he had finished, I paid a visit to the other man in the affair, an older fellow called Ford. Ford wouldn't talk to me and closed the door in my face. But by then I had my story, and I set out for home.

The next morning, I went up to the British Museum in London to see the treasure that Gordon Butcher had found. It was fabulous. I got the shivers all over again just from looking at it.

I wrote the story as truthfully as I possibly could and sent it off to

America. It was bought by *The Saturday Evening Post,* and I was well paid. When the money arrived, I sent exactly half of it to Gordon Butcher in Mildenhall.

One week later, I received a letter from Mr. Butcher written upon what must have been a page torn from a child's school exercise book. It said in part, "... you could have knocked me over with a feather when I saw your check. It was lovely. I want to thank you ..."

Here is the story almost exactly as it was written thirty years ago. I've changed it very little. I've simply toned down some of the more flowery passages and taken out a number of superfluous adjectives and unnecessary sentences.

ROALD DAHL, 1977

AROUND seven o'clock in the morning, Gordon Butcher got out of bed and switched on the light. He walked barefoot to the window and drew back the curtains and looked out.

This was January, so it was still dark, but he could tell there hadn't been any snow in the night.

"That wind," he said aloud to his wife. "Just listen to that wind."

His wife was out of bed now, standing beside him near the window, and the two of them were silent, listening to the swish and whisk of the icy wind as it came sweeping in over the fens.

"It's a nor'easter," he said.

"There'll be snow for certain before nightfall," she told him. "And plenty of it."

She was dressed before him, and she went into the next room and leaned over the cot of her six-year-old daughter and gave her a kiss. She called out a good morning to the two older children in the third room, then she went downstairs to make breakfast.

At a quarter to eight, Gordon Butcher put on his coat, his cap, and his leather gloves and walked out the back door into the bitter early-morning winter weather. As he moved through the half-daylight over the yard to the shed where his bicycle stood, the wind was like a knife on his cheek. He wheeled out the bike and mounted and began to ride down the middle of the narrow road, right into the face of the gale.

Gordon Butcher was thirty-eight. He was not an ordinary farm laborer. He took orders from no man unless he wished. He owned his own tractor, and with this he plowed other men's fields and gathered other men's harvests under contract. His thoughts were only for his wife, his son, his two daughters. His wealth was in his small brick house, his two cows, his tractor, his skill as a plowman.

GORDON
BUTCHER

Gordon Butcher's head was very curiously shaped, the back of it protruding like the sharp end of an enormous egg, and his ears stuck out, and a front tooth was missing on the left side. But none of this seemed to matter very much when you met him face to face in the open air. He looked at you with steady blue eyes that were without any malice or cunning or greed. And the mouth didn't have those thin lines of bitterness around the edges that one so often sees on men who work the land and spend their days fighting the weather.

His only eccentricity, to which he would cheerfully admit if you asked him, was in talking aloud to himself when he was alone. This habit, he said, grew from the fact that the kind of work he did left him entirely by himself for ten hours a day, six days a week. "It keeps me company," he said, "hearing me own voice now and again."

He biked on down the road, pedaling hard against the brutal wind.

"All right," he said, "all right, why don't you blow a bit? Is that the best you can do? My goodness me, I hardly know you're there this morning!"

The wind howled around him and snapped at his coat and squeezed its way through the pores of the heavy wool, through his jacket underneath, through his shirt and vest, and it touched his bare skin with an icy fingertip. "Why," he said, "it's lukewarm you are today. You'll have to do a sight better than that if you're going to make *me* shiver."

And now the darkness was diluting into a pale gray morning light, and Gordon Butcher could see the cloudy roof of the sky very low above his head and flying with the wind. Gray-blue the clouds were, flecked here

and there with black, a solid mass from horizon to horizon, the whole
thing moving with the wind, sliding past above his head like a great
gray sheet of metal unrolling. All around him lay the bleak and
lonely fen country of Suffolk, mile upon mile of it that went on
forever.

He pedaled on. He rode through the outskirts of the little
town of Mildenhall and headed for the village of West
Row, where the man called Ford had his place.

He had left his tractor at Ford's the day before because his next job was to plow up four and a half acres on Thistley Green for Ford. It was not Ford's land. It is important to remember this, but Ford was the one who had asked him to do the work.

Actually, a farmer called Rolfe owned the four and a half acres.

Rolfe had asked Ford to get it plowed because Ford, like Gordon Butcher, did plowing jobs for other men. The difference between Ford and Gordon Butcher was that Ford was somewhat grander.

He was a fairly prosperous small-time agricultural engineer who had a nice house and a large yard full of sheds filled with farm implements and machinery. Gordon Butcher had only his one tractor.

On this occasion, however, when Rolfe had asked Ford to plow up his four and a half acres on Thistley Green, Ford was too busy to do the work, so he hired Gordon Butcher to do it for him.

There was no one about in Ford's yard when Butcher rode in. He parked his bike, filled up his tractor with kerosene and gasoline, warmed the engine, hitched the plow behind, mounted the high seat, and drove out to Thistley Green.

The field was not half a mile away, and around eight-thirty Butcher drove the tractor in through the gate onto the field itself. Thistley Green was maybe a hundred acres all told, with a low hedge running around it. And although it was actually one large field, different parts of it were owned by different men. These separate parts were easy to define because each was cultivated in its own way. Rolfe's plot of four and a half acres was over to one side near the southern boundary fence. Butcher knew where it was and drove his tractor around the edge of the field, then inward until he was on the plot.

The plot was barley stubble now, covered with the short and rotting yellow stalks of barley harvested last autumn, and only recently it had been broad-sheared, so that now it was ready for the plow.

"Deep-plow it," Ford had said to Butcher the day before. "It's for sugar beet. Rolfe's putting sugar beet in there."

They only plow about four inches deep for barley, but for sugar beet they plow deep, to ten or twelve inches. A horse-drawn plow can't plow as deep as that. It was only since motor-tractors came along that the farmers had been able to deep-plow properly. Rolfe's land had been deep-plowed for sugar beet some years before this, but it wasn't Butcher who had done the plowing, and no doubt the job had been skimped a bit and the plowman had not gone quite as deep as he should. Had he done so, what was about to happen today would probably have happened then, and that would have been a different story.

Gordon Butcher began to plow. Up and down the field he went, lowering the plow deeper and deeper each trip until at last it was cutting twelve inches into the ground and turning up a smooth, even wave of black earth as it went.

The wind was coming faster now, rushing in from the killer sea, sweeping over the flat Norfolk fields, past Saxthorpe and Reepham and Honingham and Swaffham and Larling and over the border to Suffolk, to Mildenhall and to Thistley Green, where Gordon Butcher sat upright on the seat of his tractor, driving back and forth over the plot of yellow barley stubble that belonged to Rolfe. Gordon Butcher could smell the sharp crisp smell of snow not far away. He could see the low roof of the sky— no longer flecked with black, but pale and whitish gray—sliding by overhead like a solid sheet of metal unrolling.

"Well," he said, raising his voice above the clatter of the tractor, "you are surely angry at somebody today. What an almighty fuss it is now of blowin' and whistlin' and freezin'. Like a woman," he added. "Just like a woman does sometimes in the evening." And he kept his eye upon the line of the furrow, and he smiled.

At noon he stopped the tractor, dismounted, and fished in his pocket for his lunch. He found it and sat on the ground in the lee of one of the huge tractor wheels. He ate large pieces of bread and very small pieces of cheese. He had nothing to drink, for his only Thermos had got smashed by the jolting of the tractor two weeks before, and in wartime, for this was in January 1942, you could not buy another anywhere. For about fifteen minutes he sat on the ground in the shelter of the wheel and ate his lunch. Then he got up and examined his peg.

Unlike many plowmen, Butcher always hitched his plow to the tractor with a wooden peg so that if the plow fouled a root or a large stone, the peg would simply break at once, leaving the plow behind and saving the plowshares from serious damage. All over the black fen country, just below the surface, lie enormous trunks of ancient oak trees, and a wooden peg will save a plowshare many times a week out there. Although Thistley Green was well-cultivated land, field land, not fen land, Butcher was taking no chances with his plow.

He examined the wooden peg, found it sound, mounted the tractor again, and went on with his plowing.

The tractor nosed back and forth over the ground, leaving a smooth black wave of soil behind it. And still the wind blew colder, but it did not snow.

Around three o'clock, the thing happened.

There was a slight jolt, the wooden peg broke, and the tractor left the plow behind. Butcher stopped, dismounted, and walked back to the plow to see what it had struck. It was surprising for this to have happened here, on field land. There should be no oak trees underneath the soil in this place.

He knelt down beside the plow and began to scoop the soil away around the point of the plowshare. The lower tip of the share was twelve inches down. There was a lot of soil to be scooped up. He dug his gloved fingers into the earth and scooped it out with both hands. Six inches down . . . eight inches . . . ten inches . . . twelve. He slid his fingers along the blade of the plowshare until they reached the forward point of it.

The soil was loose and crumbly, and it kept falling
back into the hole he was digging. He could not
therefore see the twelve-inch-deep point of
the share. He could only feel it. And
now he could feel that the point
was indeed lodged against
something solid. He scooped away
more earth. He enlarged the hole.

It was necessary to see clearly what sort of an obstacle he had struck. If it was fairly small, then perhaps he could dig it out with his hands and get on with the job. If it was a tree trunk, he would have to go back to Ford's and fetch a spade.

"Come on," he said aloud. "I'll have you out of there, you hidden demon, you rotten old thing." And suddenly, as the gloved fingers scraped away a final handful of black earth, he caught sight of the curved rim of something flat, like the rim of a huge thick plate, sticking up out of the soil. He rubbed the rim with his fingers, and he rubbed again. Then all at once, the rim gave off a greenish glint, and Gordon Butcher bent his head closer and closer still, peering down into the little hole he had dug with his hands. For one last time, he rubbed the rim clean with his fingers, and in a flash of light, he saw clearly the unmistakable blue-green crust of ancient buried metal, and his heart stood still.

It should be explained here that farmers in this part of Suffolk, and particularly in the Mildenhall area, have for years been turning up ancient objects from the soil. Flint arrowheads from very long ago have been found in considerable numbers, but more interesting than that, Roman pottery and Roman implements have also been found. It is known that the Romans favored this part of the country during their occupation of Britain, and all local farmers are therefore well aware of the possibility of finding something interesting during a day's work. And so there was a kind of permanent awareness among Mildenhall people of the presence of treasure underneath the earth of their land.

Gordon Butcher's reaction, as soon as he saw the rim of that enormous plate, was a curious one. He immediately drew away. Then he got to his feet and turned his back on what he had just seen. He paused only long enough to switch off the engine of his tractor before he walked off fast in the direction of the road.

He did not know precisely what impulse caused him to stop digging and walk away. He will tell you that the only thing he can remember about those first few seconds was the whiff of danger that came to him from that little patch of greenish blue. The moment he touched it with his fingers, something electric went through his body, and there came to him a powerful premonition that this was a thing that could destroy the peace and happiness of many people.

In the beginning, all he had wished was to be away from it, to leave it behind him and be done with it forever. But after he had gone a hundred yards or so, he began to slow his pace. At the gate leading out from Thistley Green, he stopped.

"What in the world is the matter with you, Mr. Gordon Butcher?" he said aloud to the howling wind. "Are you frightened or something? No, I'm not frightened. But I'll tell you straight, I'm not keen to handle this alone."

That was when he thought of Ford.

He thought of Ford at first because it was for him that he was working.

He thought of him secondly because he knew that Ford was a kind of collector of old stuff, of all the old stones and arrowheads that people kept digging up from time to time in the district, which they brought to Ford and which Ford placed upon the mantel in his parlor. It was believed that Ford sold these things, but no one knew or cared how he did it.

Gordon Butcher turned toward Ford's place and walked fast out of the gate onto the narrow road, down the road around the sharp left-hand corner, and so to the house. He found Ford in his large shed, bending over a damaged harrow, mending it. Butcher stood by the door and said, "Mr. Ford!"

Ford looked around without straightening his body.

"Well, Gordon," he said, "what is it?"

Ford was middle-aged or a little older, bald-headed, long-nosed, with a clever foxy look about his face. His mouth was thin and sour, and when he looked at you, and when you saw the tightness of his mouth and the thin sour line of his lips, you knew that this was a mouth that never smiled. His chin receded, his nose was long and sharp, and he had the air about him of a sour old crafty fox from the woods.

"What is it?" he said, looking up from the harrow.

Gordon Butcher stood by the door, blue-cheeked with cold, a little out of breath, rubbing his hands slowly one against the other.

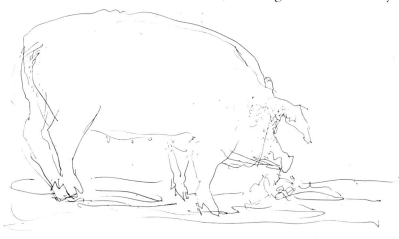

"The tractor left the plow behind," he said quietly. "There's metal down there. I saw it."

Ford's head gave a jerk. "What kind of metal?" he said sharply.

"Flat. Quite flat like a sort of huge plate."

"You didn't dig it out?" Ford had straightened up now, and there was a glint of eagles in his eyes.

Butcher said, "No, I left it alone and came straight on here."

Ford walked quickly over to the corner and took his coat off the nail. He found a cap and gloves, then he found a spade and went toward the door. There was something odd, he noticed, in Butcher's manner.

"You're sure it was metal?"

"Crusted up," Butcher said. "But it was metal all right."

"How deep?"

"Twelve inches down. At least the top of it was twelve inches down. The rest is deeper."

"How d'you know it was a plate?"

"I don't," Butcher said. "I only saw a little bit of the rim. But it looked like a plate to me. An enormous plate."

Ford's foxy face went quite white with excitement. "Come on," he said. "We'll go back and see."

The two men walked out of the shed into the fierce, ever-mounting fury of the wind. Ford shivered.

"Curse this filthy weather," he said. "Curse and blast this filthy freezing weather." And he sank his pointed foxy face deep into the collar of his coat and began to ponder upon the possibilities of Butcher's find.

One thing Ford knew that Butcher did not know. He knew that back in 1932 a man called Lethbridge, a lecturer in Anglo-Saxon antiquities at Cambridge University, had been excavating in the district and that he had actually unearthed the foundations of a Roman villa on Thistley Green itself. Ford was not forgetting that, and he quickened his pace. Butcher walked beside him without speaking, and soon they were there. They went through the gate and over the field to the plow, which lay about ten yards behind the tractor.

Ford knelt down beside the front of the plow and peered into the small hole Gordon Butcher had dug with his hands. He touched the rim of green-blue metal with a gloved finger. He scraped away a bit more earth. He leaned farther forward so that his pointed nose was right down the hole. He ran his fingers over the rough green surface. Then he stood up and said, "Let's get the plow out of the way and do some digging." Although there were fireworks exploding in his head and shivers running all over his body, Ford kept his voice very soft and casual.

Between them they pulled the plow back a couple of yards.

"Give me the spade," Ford said, and he began cautiously to dig the soil away in a circle about three feet in diameter around the exposed patch of metal. When the hole was two feet deep, he threw away the spade and used his hands. He knelt down and scraped the soil away, and gradually the little patch of metal grew and grew until at last there lay exposed before them the great round disk of an enormous plate. It was fully twenty-four inches in diameter. The lower point of the plow had just caught the raised center rim of the plate, for one could see the dent.

Carefully, Ford lifted it out of the hole. He got to his feet and stood wiping the soil away from it, turning it over and over in his hands. There was nothing much to see, for the whole surface was crusted over with a thick layer of a hard greenish blue substance. But he knew that it was an enormous plate or dish of great weight and thickness. It weighed about eighteen pounds!

Ford stood in the field of yellow barley stubble and gazed at the huge plate. His hands began to shake. A tremendous and almost unbearable excitement started boiling up inside him, and it was not easy for him to hide it. But he did his best.

"Some sort of a dish," he said.

Butcher was kneeling on the ground beside the hole. "Must be pretty old," he said.

"Could be old," Ford said. "But it's all rusted up and eaten away."

"That don't look like rust to me," Butcher said. "That greenish stuff isn't rust. It's something else."

"It's green rust," Ford said rather superbly, and that ended the discussion.

Butcher, still on his knees, was poking about casually in the now three-foot-wide hole with his gloved hands. "There's another one down here," he said.

Instantly, Ford laid the great dish on the ground. He knelt beside Butcher, and within minutes they had unearthed a second large green-encrusted plate. This one was a shade smaller than the first, and deeper. More of a bowl than a dish.

Ford stood up and held the new find in his hands. Another heavy one. And now he knew for certain they were onto something absolutely tremendous. They were onto Roman treasure, and almost without question it was pure silver. Two things pointed to its being pure silver. First, the weight, and second, the particular type of green crust caused by oxidation.

How often is a piece of Roman silver discovered in the world?

Almost never anymore.

And had pieces as large as this *ever* been unearthed before?

Ford wasn't sure, but he very much doubted it.

Worth millions it must be.

Worth literally millions of pounds.

His breath, coming fast, was making little white clouds in the freezing atmosphere.

"There's still more down here, Mr. Ford," Butcher was saying. "I can feel bits of it all over the place. You'll need the spade again."

The third piece they got out was another large plate, somewhat similar to the first. Ford placed it in the barley stubble with the other two.

Then Butcher felt the first flake of snow upon his cheek, and he looked up and saw over to the northeast a great white curtain drawn across the sky, a solid wall of snow flying forward on the wings of the wind.

"Here she comes!" he said, and Ford looked around and saw the snow moving down upon them and said, "It's a blizzard. It's a filthy, stinking blizzard!"

The two men stared at the blizzard as it raced across the fens toward them. Then it was on them, and all around was snow and snowflakes, white wind with snowflakes slanting in the wind and snowflakes in the eyes and ears and mouth and down the neck and all around. And when Butcher glanced down at the ground a few seconds later, it was already white.

"That's all we want," Ford said. "A filthy, rotten, stinking blizzard." And he shivered and sunk his sharp and foxy face deeper into the collar of his coat. "Come on," he said. "See if there's any more."

Butcher knelt down again and poked around in the soil, then in the slow and casual manner of a man having a lucky dip in a barrel of sawdust, he pulled out another plate and held it out to Ford, who took it and put it down beside the rest. Now Ford knelt down beside Butcher and began to dip into the soil with him.

For a whole hour, the two men stayed out there digging and scratching in that three-foot patch of soil. And during that hour, they found and laid upon the ground beside them *no less than thirty-four separate pieces!* There were dishes, bowls, goblets, spoons, ladles, and several other things, all of them crusted over but each one recognizable for what it was. And all the while the blizzard swirled around them and the snow gathered in little mounds upon their caps and on their shoulders and the flakes melted on

their faces so that rivers of icy water trickled down their necks. A large globule of half-frozen liquid dangled continually, like a snowdrop, from the end of Ford's pointed nose.

They worked in silence. It was too cold to speak. And as one precious article after the other was unearthed, Ford laid them carefully on the ground in rows, pausing every now and then to wipe the snow away from a dish or a spoon that was in danger of being completely covered.

At last Ford said, "That's the lot, I think."

"Yes."

Ford stood up and stamped his feet on the ground. "Got a sack in the tractor?" he said, and while Butcher walked over to fetch the sack, he turned and gazed upon the thirty-four pieces lying in the snow at his feet. He counted them again. If they were silver, which they surely must be, and if they were Roman, which they undoubtedly were, then this was a discovery that would rock the world.

Butcher called to him from the tractor, "It's only a dirty old sack."

"It'll do."

Butcher brought the sack over and held it open while Ford carefully put the articles into it. They all went in except one. The massive two-foot plate was too large for the neck of the sack.

The two men were really cold now. For over an hour they had knelt and scratched about out there in the open field with the blizzard swirling around them. Already, nearly six inches of snow had fallen. Butcher was half-frozen.

His cheeks were dead white, blotched with blue; his feet were numb like wood; and when he moved his legs, he could not feel the ground beneath him. He was much colder than Ford. Butcher's coat and clothes were not so thick, and ever since early morning he had been sitting high up on the seat of the tractor, exposed to the bitter wind. His blue-white face was tight and unmoving. All he wanted was to get home to his family and to the fire that he knew would be burning in the grate.

Ford, on the other hand, was not thinking about the cold. His mind was concentrated solely upon one thing—how to get possession of this fabulous treasure. His position, as he knew very well, was not a strong one.

In England, there is a very curious law about finding any kind of gold or silver treasure. This law goes back hundreds of years and is still strictly enforced today. The law states that if a person digs up out of the ground, even out of his own garden, a piece of metal that is either *gold* or *silver,* it automatically becomes what is known as Treasure Trove and is the property of the Crown. *The Crown* doesn't in these days mean the actual king or queen. It means the country or the government. The law also states that it is a criminal offense to conceal such a find. You are simply not allowed to hide the stuff and keep it for yourself. You must report it at once, preferably to the police. And if you do report it at once, you as the finder will be entitled to receive from the government in money the full amount of the market value of the article.

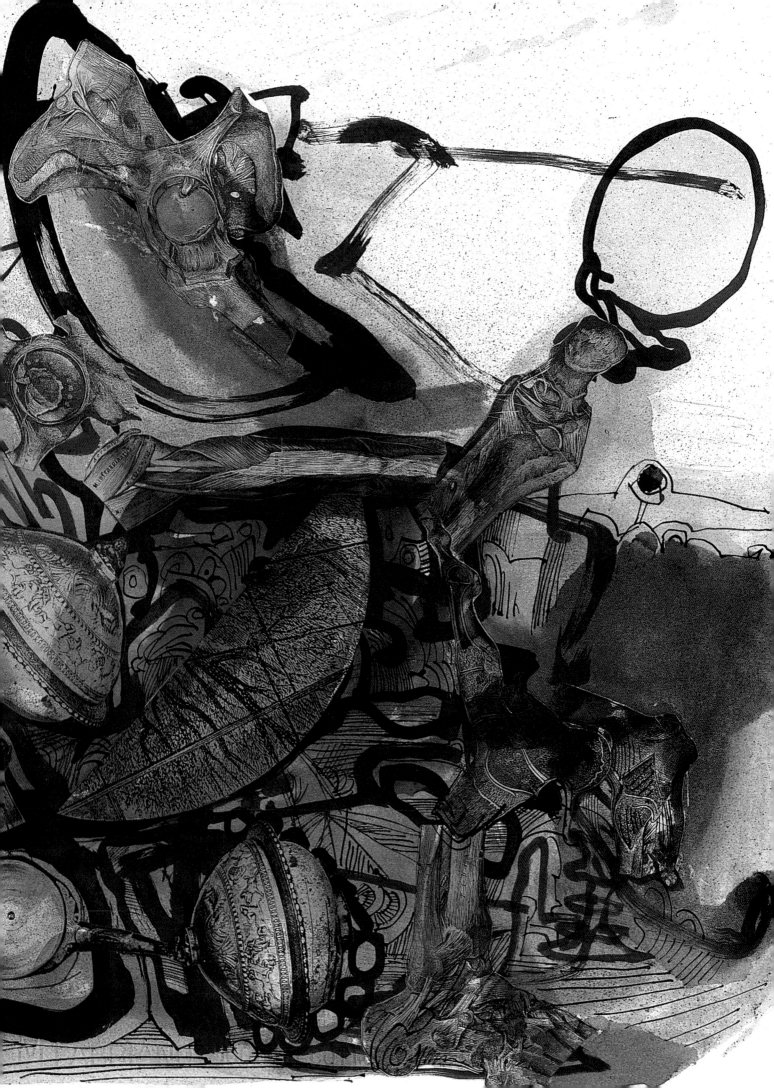

You are not required to report the digging up of other metals. You are allowed to find as much valuable pewter, bronze, copper, or even platinum as you wish, and you can keep it all; but not gold or silver.

The other curious part of this curious law is this: it is the person who *discovers* the treasure in the first place who gets the reward from the government. The owner of the land gets nothing—unless of course the finder is trespassing on the land when he makes the discovery. But if the finder of the treasure has been hired by the owner to do a job on his land, then he, the finder, gets all the reward.

In this case, the finder was Gordon Butcher. Furthermore, he was not trespassing. He was performing a job that he had been hired to do. This treasure therefore belonged to Butcher and to no one else. All he had to do was take it and show it to an expert, who would immediately identify it as silver, then turn it in to the police. In time, he would receive from the government 100 percent of its value—perhaps a million pounds sterling.

All this left Ford out in the cold, and Ford knew it. He had no rights whatsoever to the treasure by law. Thus, as he must have told himself at the time, his only chance of getting hold of the stuff for himself lay in the fact that Butcher was an ignorant man who didn't know the law and who did not anyway have the faintest idea of the value of the find. The probability was that in a few days Butcher would forget all about it. He was too simple-minded a fellow, too artless, too trusting, too unselfish to give the matter much thought.

Now, out there in the desolate snow-swept field, Ford bent down and took hold of the huge dish with one hand. He raised it but he did not lift it. The lower rim remained resting in the snow. With his other hand, he grasped the top of the sack. He didn't lift that either. He just held it. And there he stooped amid the swirling snowflakes, both hands embracing, as it were, the treasure, but not actually taking it. It was a subtle and a canny gesture. It managed somehow to signify ownership before ownership had been discussed. A child plays the same game when he reaches out and closes his fingers over the biggest chocolate éclair on the plate and then says, "Can I have this one, Mummy?" He's already got it.

"Well, Gordon," Ford said, stooping over, holding the sack and the great dish in his gloved fingers. "I don't suppose you want any of this old stuff."

It was not a question. It was a statement of fact framed as a question.

The blizzard was still raging. The snow was falling so densely, the two men could hardly see one another.

"You ought to get along home and warm yourself up," Ford went on. "You look frozen to death."

"I *feel* frozen to death," Butcher said.

"Then you get on that tractor quick and hurry home," said the thoughtful, kindhearted Ford. "Leave the plow here and leave your bike at my place. The important thing is to get back and warm yourself up before you catch pneumonia."

"I think that's just what I will do, Mr. Ford," Butcher said. "Can you manage all right with that sack? It's mighty heavy."

"I might not even bother about it today," Ford said casually. "I just might leave it here and come back for it another time. Rusty old stuff."

"So long then, Mr. Ford."

"Bye, Gordon."

Gordon Butcher mounted the tractor and drove away into the blizzard.

Ford hoisted the sack onto his shoulder, and then, not without difficulty, he lifted the massive dish with his other hand and tucked it under his arm.

"I am carrying," he told himself as he trudged through the snow, "I am now carrying what is probably the biggest treasure ever dug up in the whole history of England."

When Gordon Butcher came stamping and blowing through the back door of his small brick house late that afternoon, his wife was ironing by the fire. She looked up and saw his blue-white face and snow-encrusted clothes.

"My goodness, Gordon, you look froze to death!" she cried.

"I am," he said. "Help me off with these clothes, love. My fingers aren't hardly working at all."

She took off his gloves, his coat, his jacket, his wet shirt. She pulled off his boots and socks. She fetched a towel and rubbed his chest and shoulders vigorously all over to restore the circulation. She rubbed his feet.

"Sit down there by the fire," she said, "and I'll get you a hot cup of tea."

Later, when he was settled comfortably in the warmth with dry clothes on his back and the mug of tea in his hand, he told her what had happened that afternoon.

"He's a foxy one, that Mr. Ford," she said, not looking up from her ironing. "I never did like him."

"He got pretty excited about it all, I can tell you that," Gordon Butcher said. "Jumpy as a jackrabbit he was."

"That may be," she said. "But you ought to have had more sense than to go crawling about on your hands and knees in a freezing

blizzard just because Mr. Ford said to do it."

"I'm all right," Gordon Butcher said. "I'm warming up nicely now."

And that, believe it or not, was about the last time the subject of the treasure was discussed in the Butcher household for some years.

The reader should be reminded here that this was wartime, 1942. Britain was totally absorbed in the desperate war against Hitler and Mussolini. Germany was bombing England, and England was bombing Germany, and nearly every night Gordon Butcher heard the roar of engines from the big air base at nearby Mildenhall as the bombers took off for Hamburg, Berlin, Kiel, Wilhelmshaven, or Frankfurt. Sometimes he would wake in the early hours and hear them coming home, and sometimes the Germans flew over to bomb the base, and the Butcher house would shake with the crumph and crash of bombs not far away.

Butcher himself was exempt from military service. He was a farmer, a skilled plowman, and they had told him when he volunteered for the army in 1939 that he was not wanted. The island's food supplies must be kept going, they said, and it was vital that men like him stay on their jobs and cultivate the land.

Ford, being in the same business, was also exempt. He was a bachelor, living alone, and he was thus able to live a secret life and do secret things within the walls of his home.

And so, on that terrible snowy afternoon when they dug up the treasure, Ford carried it home and laid everything out on a table in the back room.

Thirty-four separate pieces! They covered the entire table. And by the look of it, they were in marvelous condition. Silver does not rust. The green crust of oxidation can even be a protection for the surface of the metal underneath. And with care, it could all be removed.

Ford decided to use an ordinary domestic silver polish known as Silvo, and he bought a large stock of it from the ironmonger's shop in Mildenhall. Then he took first the great two-foot plate, which weighed more than eighteen pounds. He worked on it in the evenings. He soaked it all over with Silvo. He rubbed and rubbed. He worked patiently on this single dish every night for more than sixteen weeks.

At last, one memorable evening, there showed beneath his rubbing a small area of shining silver, and on the silver, raised up and beautifully worked, there was a part of a man's head.

He kept at it, and gradually the little patch of shining metal spread and spread, the blue-green crust crept outward to the edges of the plate, until finally the top surface of the great dish lay before him in its full glory, covered all over with a wondrous pattern of animals and men and many odd legendary things.

Ford was astounded by the beauty of the great plate. It was filled with life and movement. There was a fierce face with tangled hair, a dancing goat with a human head, there were men and women and animals of many kinds cavorting around the rim, and no doubt all of them told a story.

Next, he set about cleaning the reverse side of the plate. Weeks and

weeks it took. And when the work was completed and the whole plate on both sides was shining like a star, he placed it safely in the lower cupboard of his big oak sideboard and locked the cupboard door.

One by one, he tackled the remaining thirty-three pieces. A mania had taken hold of him now, a fierce compulsion to make every item shine in all its silver brilliance. He wanted to see all thirty-four pieces laid out on the big table in a dazzling array of silver. He wanted that more than anything else, and he worked desperately hard to achieve his wish.

He cleaned the two smaller dishes next, then the large fluted bowl, then the five long-handled ladles, the goblets, the wine cups, the spoons. Every single piece was cleaned with equal care and made to shine with equal brilliance; and when they were all done, two years had passed and it was 1944.

But no strangers were allowed to look. Ford discussed the matter with no man or woman, and Rolfe, the owner of the plot on Thistley Green where the treasure had been found, knew nothing except that Ford, or someone Ford had hired, had plowed his land extremely well and very deep.

One can guess why Ford hid the treasure instead of reporting it to the police as Treasure Trove. Had he reported it, it would have been taken away and Gordon Butcher would have been rewarded as the finder. Rewarded with a fortune. So the only thing Ford could do was to hang on to it and hide it in the hope, presumably, of selling it quietly to some dealer or collector at a later date.

It is possible, of course, to take a more charitable view and assume that Ford kept the treasure solely because he loved beautiful things and wanted to have them around him. No one will ever know the true answer.

Another year went by.

The war against Hitler was won.

And then, in 1946, just after Easter, there was a knock on the door of Ford's house. Ford opened it.

"Why, hello, Mr. Ford. How are you after all these years?"

"Hello, Dr. Fawcett," Ford said. "You been keeping all right?"

"I'm fine, thank you," Dr. Fawcett said. "It's been a long time, hasn't it?"

"Yes," Ford said. "That old war kept us all pretty busy."

"May I come in?" Dr. Fawcett asked.

"Of course," Ford said. "Come on in."

Dr. Hugh Alderson Fawcett was a keen and learned archaeologist who before the war had made a point of visiting Ford once a year in search of old stones or arrowheads. Ford had usually collected a batch of such items during the twelve months, and he was always willing to sell them to Fawcett. They were seldom of great value, but now and again something quite good had turned up.

"Well," said Fawcett, taking off his coat in the little hall, "well, well, well. It's been nearly seven years since I was here last."

"Yes, it's been a long time," Ford said.

Ford led him into the front room and showed him a box of flint arrowheads that had been picked up in the district. Some were good, others not so good. Fawcett picked through them and sorted them, and a deal was done.

"Nothing else?"

"No, I don't think so."

Ford wished fervently that Dr. Fawcett had never come. He wished even more fervently that he would go away.

It was at this point that Ford noticed something that made him sweat. He saw suddenly that he had left lying on the mantel over the fireplace the two most beautiful of the Roman spoons from the treasure hoard. These spoons had fascinated him because each was inscribed with the name of a Roman girl child, to whom it had been given, presumably as a christening present, by Roman parents who had been converted to Christianity. One was Pascentia, the other was Papittedo. Rather lovely names.

Ford, sweating with fear, tried to place himself between Dr. Fawcett and the mantelpiece. He might even, he thought, be able to slip the spoons into his pocket if he got the chance.

He didn't get the chance.

Perhaps Ford had polished them so well that a little flash of reflected light from the silver caught the doctor's eye. Who knows? The fact remains that Fawcett saw them. The moment he saw them, he pounced like a tiger.

"Great heavens alive!" he cried. "What are these?"

"Pewter," Ford said, sweating more than ever. "Just a couple of old pewter spoons."

"Pewter?" cried Fawcett, turning one of the spoons over in his fingers. "Pewter! You call this *pewter?*"

"That's right," Ford said. "It's pewter."

"You know what this is?" Fawcett said, his voice going high with excitement. "Shall I tell you what this *really* is?"

"You don't have to tell me," Ford said, truculent. "I know what it is. It's old pewter. And quite nice, too."

Fawcett was reading the inscription in Roman letters on the scoop of the spoon. "Papittedo!" he cried.

"What's that mean?" Ford asked him.

Fawcett picked up the other spoon. "Pascentia," he said. "Beautiful! These are the names of Roman children! And these spoons, my friend, are made of solid silver! Solid Roman silver!"

"Not possible," Ford said.

"They're magnificent!" Fawcett cried out, going into raptures. "They're perfect! They're unbelievable! Where on earth did you find them? It's most important to know where you found them! Was there anything else?" Fawcett was hopping about all over the room.

"Well . . ." Ford said, licking dry lips.

"You must report them at once!" Fawcett cried. "They're Treasure Trove!

The British Museum is going to want these and that's for certain! How long have you had them?"

"Just a little while," Ford told him.

"And *who* found them?" Fawcett asked, looking straight at him. "Did you find them yourself or did you get them from somebody else? This is vital! The finder will be able to tell us all about it!"

Ford felt the walls of the room closing in on him and he didn't quite know what to do.

"Come on, man! Surely you know where you got them! Every detail will have to come out when you hand them in. Promise me you'll go to the police with them at once!"

"Well . . ." Ford said.

"If you don't, then I'm afraid I shall be forced to report it myself," Fawcett told him. "It's my duty."

The game was up now, and Ford knew it. A thousand questions would be asked. How did you find it? When did you find it? What were you doing? Where was the exact spot? Whose land were you plowing? And sooner or later, inevitably, the name of Gordon Butcher would have to come into it. It was unavoidable. And then, when Butcher was questioned, he would remember the size of the hoard and tell them all about it.

So the game was up. And the only thing to do at this point was to unlock the doors of the big sideboard and show the entire hoard to Dr. Fawcett.

Ford's excuse for keeping it all and not turning it in would have to be that he thought it was pewter. So long as he stuck to that, he told himself, they couldn't do anything to him.

Dr. Fawcett would probably have a heart attack when he saw what there was in that cupboard.

"There is actually quite a bit more of it," Ford said.

"Where?" cried Fawcett, spinning around. "Where, man, where? Lead me to it!"

"I really thought it was pewter," Ford said, moving slowly and very reluctantly forward to the oak sideboard. "Otherwise, I would naturally have reported it at once."

He bent down and unlocked the lower doors of the sideboard. He opened the doors.

And then Dr. Hugh Alderson Fawcett very nearly did have a heart attack. He flung himself on his knees. He gasped. He choked. He began spluttering like an old kettle. He reached out for the great silver dish. He took it. He held it in shaking hands and his face went as white as snow. He didn't speak. He couldn't. He was literally—physically and mentally—struck absolutely dumb by the sight of the treasure.

The interesting part of the story ends here. The rest is routine. Ford went to Mildenhall Police Station and made a report. The police came at once and collected all thirty-four pieces, and they were sent under guard to the British Museum for examination.

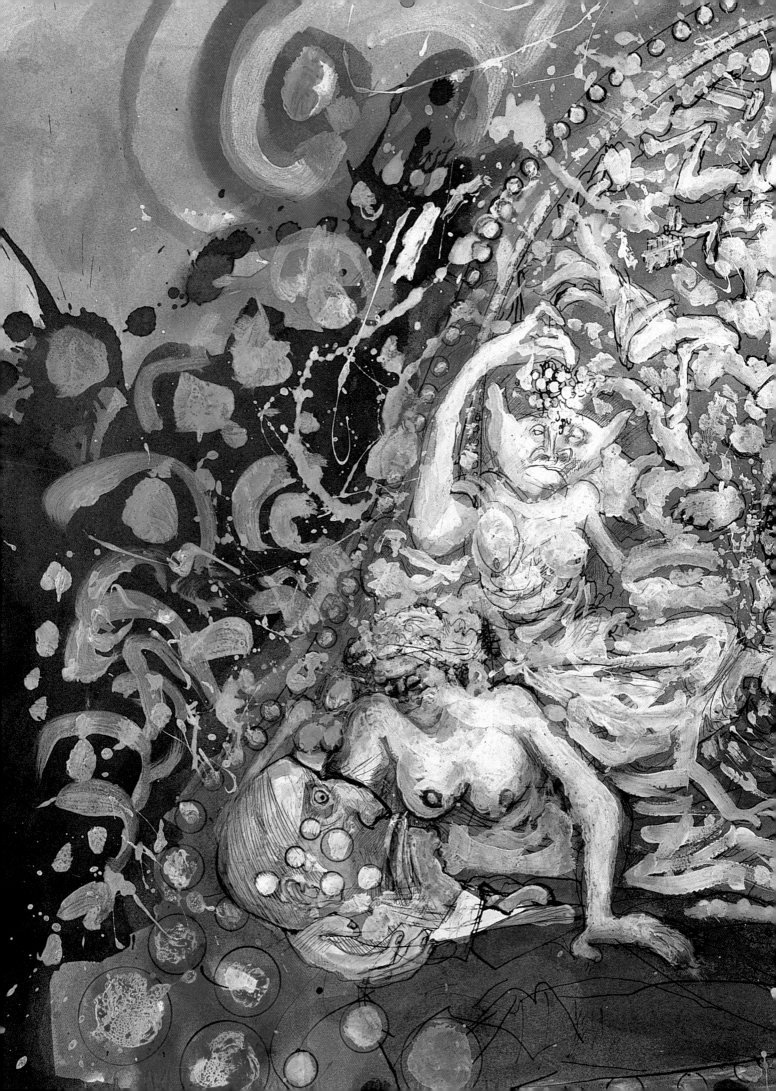

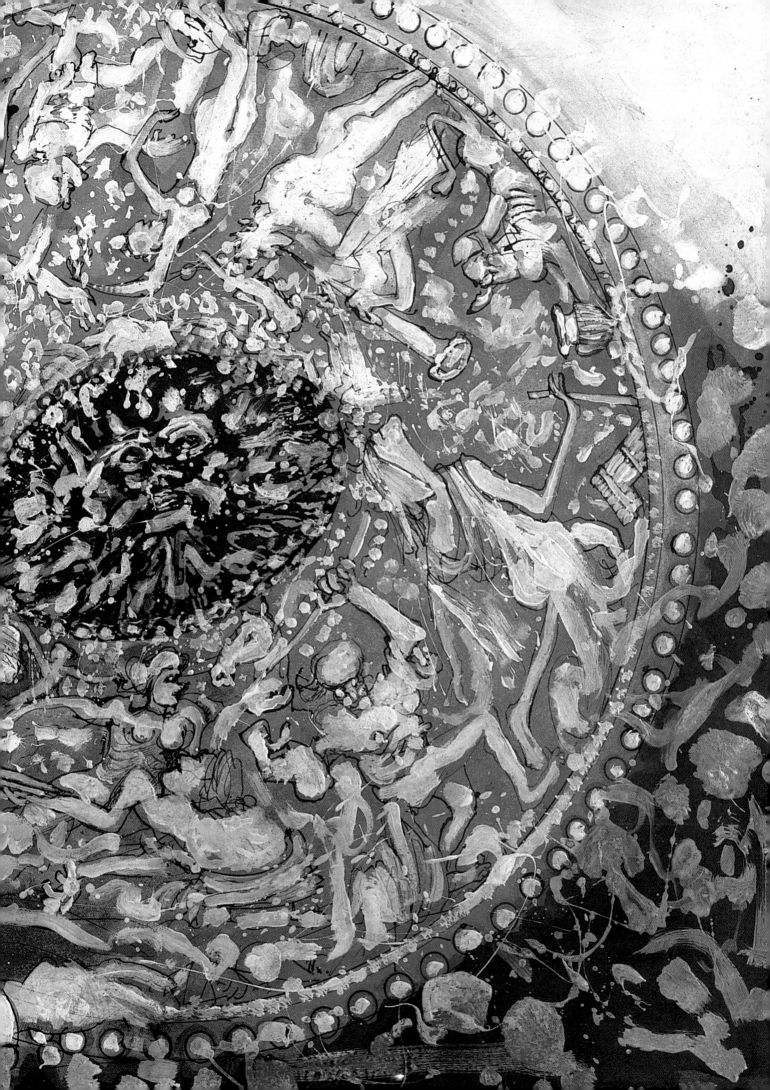

Then an urgent message came from the Museum to the Mildenhall police. It was far and away the finest Roman silver ever found in the British Isles. It was of enormous value. The Museum (which is really a public governmental institution) wished to acquire it. In fact, they insisted upon acquiring it.

The wheels of the law began to turn. An official inquest and hearing was arranged at the nearest large town, Bury St. Edmunds. The silver was moved there under special police guard. Ford was summoned to appear before the coroner and a jury of fourteen, while Gordon Butcher, that good and quiet man, was ordered also to present himself to give evidence.

On Monday, July 1, 1946, the hearing took place, and the coroner cross-questioned Ford closely.

"You thought it was pewter?"

"Yes."

"Even after you had cleaned it?"

"Yes."

"You took no steps to inform any experts of the find?"

"No."

"What did you intend to do with the articles?"

"Nothing. Just keep them."

And when he had concluded his evidence, Ford asked permission to go outside into the fresh air because he said he felt faint. Nobody was surprised.

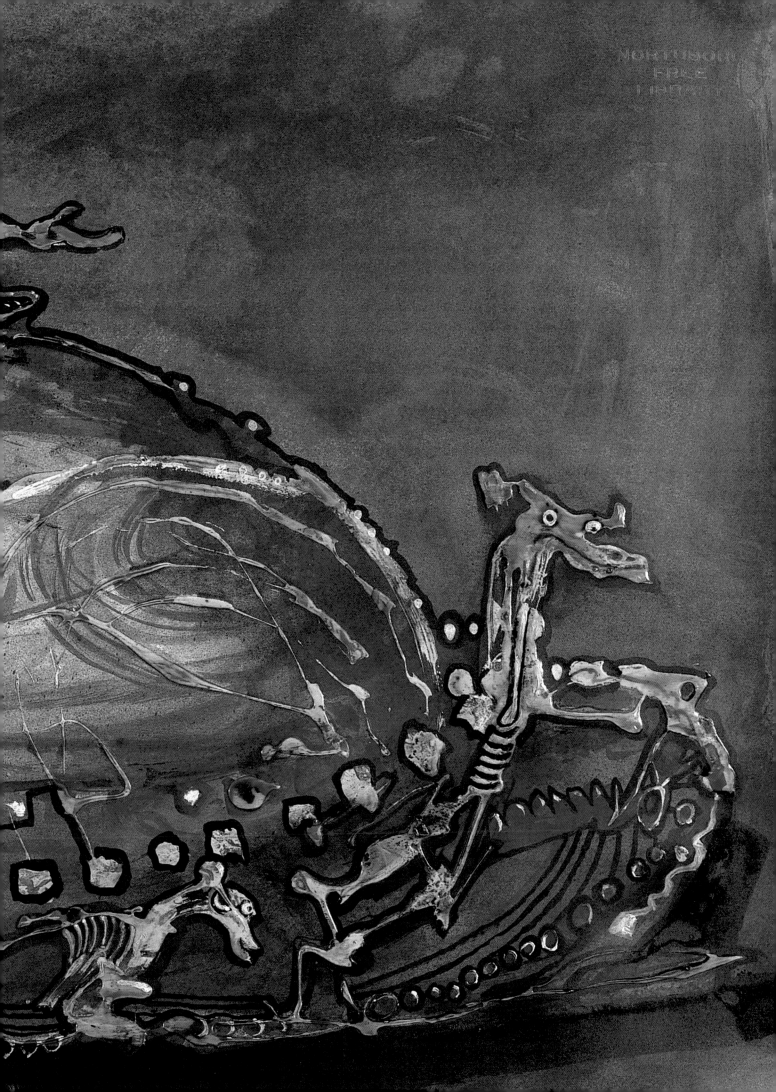
NORTHPORT
FREE
LIBRARY

Then Butcher was called, and in a few simple words he told of his part in the affair.

Dr. Fawcett gave his evidence, as did several other learned archaeologists, all of whom testified to the extreme rarity of the treasure. They said that it was of the fourth century after Christ; that it was the table silver of a wealthy Roman family; that it had probably been buried by the owner's bailiff to save it from the Picts and Scots, who swept down from the north in about A.D. 365–67 and laid waste many Roman settlements. The man who buried it had probably been liquidated either by a Pict or by a Scot, and the treasure had remained concealed a foot below the soil ever since. The workmanship, said the experts, was magnificent. Some of it may have been executed in England, but more probably the articles were made in Italy or in Egypt. The great plate was of course the finest piece. The head in the center was that of Neptune, the sea god, with dolphins in his hair and seaweed in his beard. All around him, sea nymphs and sea monsters gamboled. On the broad rim of the plate stood Bacchus and his attendants. There was wine and revelry. Hercules was there, quite drunk, supported by two satyrs, his lion's skin fallen from his shoulders. Pan was there too, dancing upon his goat legs with his pipes in his hand. And everywhere there were maenads, female devotees of Bacchus, rather tipsy women.

The court was told also that several of the spoons bore the monogram of Christ (*Chi-Rho*) and that the two that were inscribed with the names Pascentia and Papittedo were undoubtedly christening presents.

The experts concluded their evidence, and the court adjourned. Soon the jury returned, and their verdict was astonishing. No blame was attached to anyone for anything, although the finder of the treasure was no longer entitled to receive full compensation from the Crown because the find had not been declared at once. Nevertheless, there would probably be a measure of compensation paid, and with this in view, the finders were declared to be jointly Ford and Butcher.

Not Butcher. Ford and Butcher.

There is no more to tell other than that the treasure was acquired by the British Museum, where it now stands proudly displayed in a large glass case for all to see. And already people have traveled great distances to go and look upon those lovely things that Gordon Butcher found beneath his plow on that cold and windy winter afternoon. One day, a book or two will be compiled about them, full of suppositions and abstruse conclusions, and men who move in archaeological circles will talk forever about the Treasure of Mildenhall.

As a gesture, the Museum rewarded the co-finders with one thousand pounds each. Butcher, the true finder, was happy and surprised to receive so much money. He did not realize that, had he been allowed to take the treasure home originally, he would almost certainly have revealed its existence and would thus have become eligible to receive 100 percent of its value, which could have been anything between half a million and a million pounds.

Nobody knows what Ford thought about it all. He must have been relieved and perhaps somewhat surprised when he heard that the court had believed his story about pewter. But above all, he must have been shattered by the loss of his great treasure. For the rest of his life he would be kicking himself for leaving those two spoons on the mantel above the fireplace for Dr. Fawcett to see.

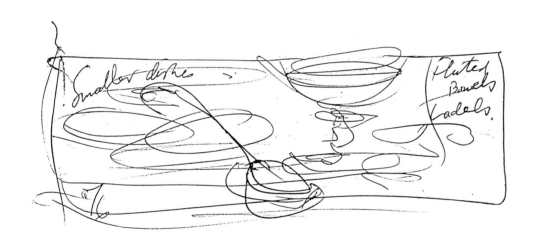